To Lexie
Just because
from Grandpa Norm
Aug 2001

A MOUSE IN SOLOMON'S HOUSE

published by Gold 'n' Honey Books — *a part of the Questar publishing family*

©1995 by Questar Publishers
Illustrations ©1995 by Normand Chartier

Design by David Uttley

International Standard Book Number: 0-88070-771-2

Printed in the United States of America

For information:
Questar Publishers, Inc. • Post Office Box 1720 • Sisters, Oregon 97759

95 96 97 98   99 00 01 02 — 10 9 8 7 6 5 4 3 2 1

A CHILD'S BOOK OF WISDOM

A MOUSE IN SOLOMON'S HOUSE

By Mack Thomas
Illustrated by Normand Chartier

Gold 'n' Honey
BOOKS

CHAPTER ONE

Against the Wall

A Story about Wisdom

One morning a mouse named Marble
saw something wonderful: The tall cedar doors
in the front of King Solomon's palace
(where Marble lived with his mother and father
and brothers and sisters) were open wide!
Marble had never been outside before.
He looked both ways down the front hall.
No one was there. No one would see him.
So he dashed across the shiny stone floor.

A warm, sweet breeze was blowing
over the palace grounds and across the palace porch.
How very different this was from his family's home
in a little hole in a dark corner far inside the palace.
Marble wondered where the breeze came from.
Well, he thought, *there's only one way to find out.*

He scurried down the palace steps
and hurried across the palace lawn.
Then he noticed that even though the day was sunny,
he was always under a little shadow.
If he stepped to the left, the shadow went left.
If he stepped to the right, the shadow went right.

So he stopped.

The shadow got bigger. Marble looked up.

What he saw would make anyone scream.

(At least it certainly made Marble scream!)

It was a snow-white hawk,
beautiful and strong, with gleaming talons
that could tear a mouse to pieces.
"Who are you?" Marble squeaked.
"What do you want?"
The hawk spread wide her wings.
"You may call me Wisdom," she said
in a voice as deep as thunder. "And I want you!"

Marble turned and ran his very fastest.
She can fly, all right, he told himself,
but I'm quicker on the ground!
Down a slope he raced, and under a hedge,
and around a tree, and along a wall.

But where the wall turned a corner,
there she was again!
Marble tried to run back, but she stepped on his tail.
"If your parents sent you outside," she said,
"they would have told you I'm a friend.
You must have come without their permission."
Marble trembled so much he couldn't answer.
"Go and tell them you're sorry," she continued.
"Then ask if you can come out once more.
Tell them Wisdom will watch over you."

The minute she let go of Marble's tail,
he hurried back along the wall, and around the tree,
and under the hedge, and up the slope,
and over the palace lawn, and up the palace steps,
and across the palace porch, and through the doors,
and down the front hall, and all the way back
to the little hole in a dark corner far inside the palace.

"Marble, *where* have you been?"
said his mother and father and brothers and sisters.
"I'm sorry," Marble cried.
"I went outside without asking."
Marble had to spend the rest of the day
alone in his room. All afternoon,
he thought about what the hawk had said.

At suppertime he asked his parents,
"May I go outside again? Wisdom is there,
and she promised to watch over me."
"You may," said his father with a smile.
"But only if you stay in Wisdom's sight,
and do whatever Wisdom tells you."
As Marble's mother gave him honey and bread,
his father added, "If you let Wisdom be your friend,
your adventures will never end."

Marble would soon discover
that his father was absolutely right.

Whoever finds wisdom is happy.

PROVERBS 3:13

CHAPTER TWO

A House with Holes

A Story about Choosing the Right Friends

Skipping through the palace gardens,
Marble followed the flying hawk.
He was jumping with excitement.
"When we prayed at home last night,"
he shouted, "Daddy told me about you.
He said, 'Love Wisdom. Stay with her, Marble.
Call her your friend, and she'll take care of you.'"
The hawk smiled. "Your father is wise," she said.
"Can you tell me how he learned so much?"

They came to a shady spot. There on a garden table
they found golden apples served on a silver tray.
Marble took the biggest apple.
"Daddy told me," he said between bites,
"that God made King Solomon wise—
wiser than any man or mouse in the world.
So Daddy follows the king all around the palace.
He listens to the king's wise words. That way,
he can teach them to my brothers and sisters and me."

Just then they heard a burst of laughter.

"Sounds like a party!" shouted Marble
(who loved parties more than anything else).

He saw someone through the garden trees.

"And it *looks* like a party! Let's go!" he added,
without looking back at the hawk.

"I'm your new friend Marble," Marble said politely
to the first creature he came to. "What's your name?"

"LOUD LADY FOLLY!" she answered.

She laughed so hard it hurt Marble's ears.

"And that's MY HOUSE!" she shouted.

She threw a stone, knocking a hole in the roof.
Marble heard a noise from inside. He hurried
through the door to see if someone was hurt.

"WELCOME to the home of COOL THE FOOL!"
yelled another laughing rock-thrower inside.
Another stone came crashing through,
so Marble found a place to hide.
"Excuse me, Cool the Fool," he said politely.
"Didn't your parents ever tell you not to do this?"
"Of course," said Cool the Fool
as he threw another rock even harder.

He scooped up Marble in the basket,
and threw him out as well.
Marble landed hard on his head.
Lady Folly and Cool the Fool laughed even louder.
That was enough for Marble. He ran away.
"Wisdom!" he cried. "Wisdom! Where are you?"

He found her waiting for him,
at the table in the shady spot. He caught his breath,
and told her what had happened.
"I didn't like their party," he added.
The hawk replied, "And what wise words
would King Solomon say about that?"

"I don't know," Marble answered,
"but I'll ask my daddy."
The rest of the morning they climbed trees
(which Marble had never done before).
Then the great white hawk flew him home.

*You only get hurt
when you make friends with fools.*

PROVERBS 13:20

CHAPTER THREE

Down on the Farm

A Story about Working Hard

Marble and his brothers and sisters
were busy the next day playing in the palace.
They were climbing tapestries
and swinging on tassels
and sliding down table legs
and hiding in treasure trunks
and bouncing on the throne.

At suppertime that night, their father told them
all the wise words he heard from the king that day.
After serving everyone melon for dessert,
he prayed for each of his children by name:
for the girls—Ivory, Silk, and Jewel;
and the boys—Marble, Cedar, Silver, and Gold.
Then he said to their mother (as he always did),
"What riches we have in our house!"

The next day everyone did chores.

Marble's job was dusting.

He didn't enjoy it much anymore. After a while

he asked his mother if he could go outside again.

"Yes," she agreed—"*if* you find Wisdom,

and *if* you let Wisdom watch over you."

The hawk was waiting.
She led Marble across the palace grounds
and out the palace gate,
and across the city and out the city gate.

Marble stopped to look at ants
marching across the road. He asked the hawk,
"Where are they going? What are they doing?"
"They're working," she answered. "Gathering food,
and taking it home to keep for later."
"Do they ever stop and just have fun?" Marble asked.
"No," said the hawk. "There isn't time."

They came to a farm.

It was grown up in thorns and weeds.

In the farmhouse window, Marble saw the farmer.

"Hello! Hello!" Marble called out politely.

The farmer didn't answer or even turn his head.

Marble went closer.

The farmer was at his table, staring at his food.

This could become a party! Marble thought.

"My name is Marble," he said. "What's yours?"

Without blinking or nodding or moving at all,

the farmer slowly answered, "S-S-S-Sluggard."

Marble wondered how to get this farmer going.
"Maybe," he remarked, as he glanced out at the fields,
"you'd feel better if you worked around the farm.
You could clear away weeds and thorns,
and grow melons to serve
whenever you have a party.
After all, it *is* a nice day for working outside."
Just then, a warm, sweet breeze began blowing.
The sound rustled all around the house.

The farmer screamed:

"There's a lion outside! There's a lion outside!"

He sprang from the table

and dived under his bedcovers.

"I'll be killed!" he cried. "I'll be killed!"

"No," Marble assured him, "it's only the wind.

Don't be afraid."

But now the farmer was snoring.
Marble left him in bed and walked away
through the weeds and thorns.
"It's too bad about this farm," he told the hawk.
She answered, "Perhaps King Solomon
will have wise words about this."
Marble nodded. "I'll ask Daddy tonight," he said.

Back home, Marble first found some places to dust
that he missed earlier. Before supper,
he cleaned them better than ever.

How long will you lie there, you sluggard?…
Lazy hands will make you poor.

PROVERBS 6:9, 10:4

CHAPTER FOUR

THE HORSES AND THE PRINCE

A Story about Humility

One day Marble saw the royal horses
for the very first time.
He and the hawk spent all afternoon
at the running fields near King Solomon's stables.
As he watched the horses, Marble said to himself,
"They're so huge and so strong, and not like me.
I'm actually only a small mouse.
But if I were a prince, I could ride them."
Marble had never ridden a horse before.

"A storm is coming," the hawk warned.

She led Marble toward the stables.

On the way, he saw a peacock in a fig tree.

"Hello up there!" he called politely.

"I'm Marble. Who are you?"

The peacock stiffened his neck and said,

"Did someone forget who I am?

I—Proud Prince Mocker, big and beautiful and blue?"

"No," Marble replied. "I didn't forget. I never knew."

"Now you know," said the peacock,
flashing his feathers. "You must also know
that tomorrow I'll be even bigger and bluer
and smarter and stronger and richer than I am today."
Marble wanted to ask the prince if he ever rode horses.
But first he glanced at the sky and said,
"Perhaps you'd better get down from that fig tree.
A storm is coming."

"You must also know," stated the peacock,
"that no storm can blow until I say so.
And I have decided that today's weather
will stay wonderful and warm, with no storm."
Marble answered, "But Wisdom told me—"
The peacock angrily interrupted: "Wisdom!
Wisdom! That pale-feathered, highty-flighty
hook-beak! What does she know?"

Then the stormwind struck,
blasting the prince from the tree.
Marble saw an open stable door,
and ran inside for safety.

While waiting for the wind and rain to stop,
Marble made friends with the horses.
Soon the peacock came straggling in, looking soaked
and sore. "You horses must know," he cackled,
"that without asking *me,* you stirred up a storm—
you long-legged, broom-tailed barrel-noses!"
He strutted back and forth in the stable doorway,
calling them other names as well.

The horses paid no attention to the peacock.
When the storm had passed,
they raced out the stable door and ran right over him.
One horse gave Marble a ride
all around the running fields.

When the horse-ride was over
and Marble was on his way home,
he said to the hawk, "I'm not a horse.
And I'm glad I'm not a prince.
I'm actually only a small mouse."
He splashed in a puddle and added,
"And I'd like to be the best small mouse I can be."

The one who is proud will be destroyed,
but those who are humble will be honored.

PROVERBS 16:18, 18:12

CHAPTER FIVE

In the Marketplace

A Story about Honesty

Marble's father was building a new table.
Marble helped him. As they worked,
his father told him more of the king's wise words.
"The Lord hates lying lips," his father explained,
"but He's glad when someone tells the truth."

Later his mother called him. "Marble," she said,
"you can go to the marketplace for me today,
if Wisdom goes with you." Marble was glad.
He had never been to the marketplace before.
His mother gave him money in a basket and said,
"I need two olives to make an olive pie.
Buy me two olives, and nothing else.
And if you have no trouble, I'll let you go again."

On their way, the hawk asked Marble,
"What wise words from King Solomon
have you learned today?"
Marble remembered: "The Lord hates lying lips,"
he quoted, "but He likes it when we tell the truth."
At the marketplace, the hawk flew to the top
of a gateway nearby, to watch Marble shop.

"Excuse me," Marble said politely to some traders.
"Can you tell me where the olive merchant is?"
Marble saw the three traders wink at each other,
and tap their toes, and jiggle their fingers.
One of them grinned and said,
"The olive merchant got sick and went home.
But don't worry—we'll sell you something better
than olives! How much money do you have?"

Marble liked what they showed him, but kept quiet.

He didn't want to say how much money he had.

"Maybe you aren't sure," said another of the traders.

"Just show me your money, and I'll count it for you."

Marble stayed silent and hugged his basket close.

He stood and stared at every wonderful thing

the traders had for sale.

Suddenly he felt a sharp tug on his basket—
then it was gone. One of the traders had snatched it!
"Wisdom!" Marble yelled. "They're robbing me!"
The traders ran away, and Marble raced after them.

At once he heard a screech and a scream.
The hawk swirled and whirled upon the traders.
They fled through the city gates, howling and yowling.
On their way out, they flung Marble's basket away.

Marble hurried to pick it up. It had dropped
right beside the stall of the olive merchant!
"They told me you were sick!" Marble exclaimed.
"They lied to you," the merchant answered,
"so they could rob you."

All the way back Marble wondered,

Will I ever get to go to the marketplace again?

At home, his mother thanked him for the olives.

When she asked, "Did you have any trouble?"

Marble sat down beside her at the new table

to tell her everything. "I'm glad," he began,

"that Wisdom watched over me today...."

The Lord hates lying lips,
but He is glad when someone tells the truth.

PROVERBS 12:22

CHAPTER SIX

Alone at Night

A Story about Wisdom

The next afternoon, when Marble returned
from swimming in the royal pool,
the hawk pointed out a cat lurking on the lawn.
Marble had heard about her: It was Sphinx,
the queen's dangerous pet from Egypt.
"Stay away from her," the hawk warned.
"I will," answered Marble.

At bedtime that night Marble asked, "Daddy, why do you always tell us what King Solomon says?" Daddy answered, "Because someday you'll grow up. Someday you'll move away from your mother and me. And when your Leaving Day comes, the king's words will stay with you, to help you do everything right."

Marble took his father's hand and whispered, "I hope my Leaving Day is a long time away."

Marble couldn't get to sleep. He was thinking about all he had seen outside. He wondered: *What would it be like to be out there all the time?*

Marble had been outdoors in the daylight. But never before had he been out in the dark. What was it really like — out there — *at night?*

Well, he thought, *there's only one way to find out.*

Marble was forgetting many things
as he quietly slipped through the palace.
But on he went. He didn't turn back
even when he saw the big front doors closed.
Instead, he found an open window. Outside
in the moonlight, a cool sweet breeze was blowing.
Marble hurried across the palace grounds.
Hearing the night sounds, feeling the night feelings,
he rambled and roamed his way to the palace gate.

And there, someone leaped out upon him.
It was Sphinx! She had him by the tail.
She suddenly looked up, however,
when a rustle sounded in the tree above them.
Marble quickly gave his tail a mighty yank,
pulling it free, and ran.

Out the palace gate he sped and looked back.
Sphinx wasn't following. But she stood in the gate
and screamed, "Don't you dare come this way again!"
Marble had forgotten so much that night,
and now, all he remembered was how to run.

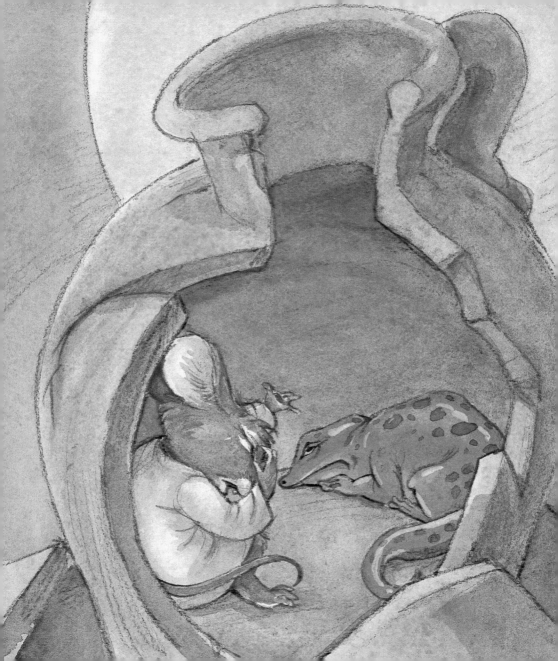

Finally, his little legs could run no longer.
He saw an old waterpot. He slipped inside.
Marble sat down by a sleeping lizard
to think and catch his breath. Soon, however,
he woke up the lizard. He wanted someone to talk to.
"I ran away from home and I shouldn't have,"
he moaned. "Oh, why did I forget so much?"
The lizard didn't care, and went back to sleep.
So Marble yelled, *"Wisdom! Wisdom, help me!"*

She must have been waiting right
beside the waterpot, because she answered at once.
On the spot,
she and Marble had a long talk about everything.
She helped him remember all that
he had forgotten.

In due time, Wisdom flew Marble home,
to that little hole in a bright corner
far inside the palace. Marble woke up his parents
and told them everything, with many tears.

IT WAS QUITE A LONG TIME before Marble
was allowed to go out again. But when he did,
he was surely about the wisest little mouse
anyone would ever meet.

Teach someone who is wise, and he'll become even wiser.
PROVERBS 9:9